Contents

Contents

Read 75

75-Word Reading Passages
for
Fact, Fiction, and Fun
at the
700-Word Level

Andrew E. Bennett

PRO LINGUA ● ASSOCIATES

Pro Lingua Associates, Publishers

P.O. Box 1348, Brattleboro, Vermont 05302 USA
Office: 802 257 7779 • Orders: 800 366 4775
Email: info@ProLinguaAssociates.com
WebStore: www.ProLinguaAssociates.com
SAN: 216-0579

At Pro Lingua
our objective is to foster an approach
to learning and teaching that we call
interplay, the interaction of language
learners and teachers with their materials,
with the language and culture,
and with each other in active, creative,
and productive play.

ISBN 0-86647-229-0

This book was written and designed by Andrew E. Bennett. The Read & Learn edition was adapted for Pro Lingua by Raymond C. Clark. The design was adjusted by Arthur A. Burrows. It was printed and bound by Worzalla in Stevens Point, Wisconsin.

Cover by James Borstein, Corporate Communications: Targeted Graphics and Design

Image Credits:

   iStock Photos – pp. 2, 6, 28, 32, 66 (© iStock Photos)
   Hemera – pp. 8, 10, 30, 64 (left), 68, 70, 72 (© Hemera)
   Corel Gallery – pp. 22, 48, 54, 58, 64 (right), 74 (© Corel)
   Corel Photos – pp. 38, 52, 80 (© Corel)
   Big Book of Art – pp. 4, 12, 17, 24, 26, 36, 40 (©Hemera)
   Qiu Ge – p. 44 (© Andrew E. Bennett)
   Julio Etchart – p 62 (www.ucar.edu)
   Art Explosion 750,000 - pp, 60, 62, 78 (©Nova Development)
   E&A – pp. 24, 36, 76 (© E&A Digital Arts)
   Xun Zi Xing & Chen Yen Ming – pp. 20, 50 (© Andrew E. Bennett)
   Upper Deck – p. 14 (Used with permission, © Upper Deck)
   Dance and Jump – p. 56 (© Dance and Jump Software)
   Andrew E. Bennett – p. 16 (© Andrew E. Bennett)

Printed in the United States of America.
First edition. First Printing 2006. 2,000 copies in print.

Dear Reader,

Welcome to Book Two in the Read and Learn Series. You can read about the world we live in -- our home and the places in it. You can read about the things we do -- work, play, travel, study, shop, talk, email, and eat. And you can learn a lot of useful English.

There are 40 units in this book. Each unit has a reading and three exercises. The units are easy to do.

- Do the reading
- Do the exercises
- Check your answers (the answers start on page 82)

But first, you should understand these instructions before you begin to work.

_____ Write the correct word in each blank.

_____ Choose the best answer.

_____ Put the words in the correct order.

_____ Complete each sentence.

_____ Match each question with the correct answer.

_____ Match each sentence with a response.

_____ Combine the two sentences into one sentence.

Now, read and learn and enjoy the book.

Pro Lingua Associates

1 Niagara Falls

Each year, millions of people visit Niagara Falls. The falls are two large waterfalls along the Niagara River. They are separated by an island. The river separates the USA and Canada. So the Falls are shared by the two friendly countries.

The first waterfall, called Horseshoe Falls, is on the Canadian side of the river. The second, called American Falls, is on the US side. Horseshoe Falls is five feet higher. Both waterfalls are very powerful.

Vocabulary

Write the correct word in each blank.

along	side	visit	high	both

1. My uncle lives in New York. I _____ him every month.

2. There are trees all _____ 5th Street. It's really beautiful.

3. Put the table on the other _____ of the room.

4. _____ of those bags are mine.

Choose the best answer.

1. (   ) Where is the Niagara River?
   A: Next to millions of cities.
   B: Near the world's largest waterfall.
   C: In between the USA and Canada.
   D: Close to Canada, but not the USA.

2. (   ) In the first paragraph, what does "separates" mean?
   A: causes problems   B: divides
   C: enters   D: is near

3. (   ) American Falls is 182 feet high. How many feet high is Horseshoe Falls?
   A: 5.   B: 177.
   C: 182.   D: 187.

4. (   ) Which of the following is true?
   A: Niagara's two falls are weak.
   B: The waterfalls are the same height.
   C: American Falls is the lower of the two falls.
   D: Horseshoe Falls and American Falls are on the same side of the river.

Grammar Put the words in the correct order.

1. Niagara River The falls are two on the
   _____.

2. very falls are Both powerful
   _____.

3. called Horseshoe Falls is The first
   _____.

4. second American Falls called is The
   _____.

2   Lucy at the Library

Lucy loves the library. It's like her second home. There are so many interesting books there. Each one has its own secrets. Each one has something to teach and share. Some have beautiful pictures. Others have interesting stories. To Lucy, books are like good friends. At the library, Lucy has friends all around her.

The staff at the library all know Lucy. They help her choose books. From time to time, Lucy helps them. She introduces other readers to good books.

Vocabulary

Write the correct word in each blank.

introduce	share	secret	choose	picture

1. Don't tell anybody my _____.

2. Let me _____ you to my good friend Chris.

3. Which color shirt should I _____?

4. Here is a _____ of me and my best friend.

Choose the best answer.

1. (   ) Why is the library like Lucy's second home?
        A: She spends a lot of time there.
        B: She sleeps there.
        C: It is next to her house.
        D: Her family members work there.

2. (   ) Lucy and the library staff _____.
        A: help each other
        B: don't know each other
        C: choose good books only for Lucy
        D: are too busy to talk to other people

3. (   ) What does "from time to time" mean?
        A: all the time   B: sometimes
        C: very often   D: almost never

4. (   ) What would Lucy say?
        A: "I hate books."
        B: "Books can teach me many things."
        C: "The library is too far away."
        D: "I rarely talk to people at the library."

Grammar

Write the correct word in each blank.

1. _____ book has something to tell.
   (Each/Some)

2. _____ have many stories to tell.
   (Some/Each)

3. _____ have only a few things to tell.
   (Each/Others)

4. _____ have something to tell.
   (All/Other)

Basketball is played by boys, girls, men, and women all over the world. To play, you need only a basketball and a court.

The basic rules of the game are simple. Just shoot the ball into the basket. Also, you can't run with the ball. You must bounce it on the court as you run.

The NBA is the world's top league. It has great players from many countries. The WNBA, the top league for women, is also full of excellent players.

Vocabulary

Write the correct word in each blank.

| excellent | rule | simple | play | country |

1. Which _____ would you like to travel to?

2. That movie was _____! I want to see it again.

3. The library has one important _____: Don't talk loudly.

4. This is a(n) _____ meal. We can make it in a few minutes.

Choose the best answer.

1. (   ) Who likes to play basketball?
   A: Only young people.
   B: Mostly older people.
   C: Boys, girls, men, and women.
   D: Men and boys only.

2. (   ) Basketball players cannot _____ the ball.
   A: run and carry   B: bounce
   C: shoot   D: hold

3. (   ) What is the WNBA?
   A: A league for women.   B: The only basketball league.
   C: A boy's league.   D: A college league.

4. (   ) Which of the following is true?
   A: The basic rules of basketball are hard to learn.
   B: There's only one basketball league for top players.
   C: You must not bounce the ball during a game.
   D: The NBA has players from outside the USA.

Grammar

Combine the two sentences into one sentence.

1. The players are tall. The players are skillful.

   _____

2. He plays basketball. He plays football.

   _____

3. Lisa plays for the Tigers. Carol plays for the Tigers.

   _____

4 New Friends

Omar: Hi, how are you?
Moshe: Pretty good, how about you?
Omar: Not bad. You're new here, aren't you?
Moshe: Yeah, I am.
Omar: So, how do you like it here at WCC?
Moshe: So far, it's pretty nice. I like the campus.
Omar: Me, too! And the computer lab is great.
Moshe: Yeah, I like it, too.
Omar: My name's Omar.
Moshe: I'm Moshe. Nice to meet you.
Omar: Same here. It's time for class. Let's meet our ESL teacher.
Moshe: OK. Let's go!

Vocabulary

Write the correct word or phrase in each blank.

| lab | so far | great | student | time |

1. Is it _____ to go?

2. _____, I'm doing OK.

3. What time does the _____ close?

4. Most of my classes are _____. I'm learning a lot.

Choose the best answer.

1. (   ) Moshe _____ his new school.
   A: misses
   B: hates
   C: studies
   D: likes

2. (   ) Omar and Moshe both like _____.
   A: the same clothes   B: the campus
   C: to dance   D: to read

3. (   ) What does "Not bad" mean?
   A: Terrible.   B: That's wrong.
   C: Well.   D: Don't say that.

4. (   ) Which of the following is true?
   A: Moshe doesn't know about the school's lab.
   B: Moshe and Omar are classmates.
   C: Omar doesn't like the computer lab.
   D: Omar is not very friendly.

Grammar

Match each question with the correct answer.

1. __ How are you?	A: At 10:30.
2. __ Where are you going?	B: Mr. Lin, I think.
3. __ What time does class start?	C: To the bathroom.
4. __ Who is the teacher?	D: Pretty good, thanks.

7:30-8:15	Wake up, brush my teeth, have breakfast
8:15	Go to school
8:30-9:25	Math class
9:30-10:25	History class
10:25-10:50	Break
10:50-11:45	Science class
11:45-12:55	Lunch
1:00-1:55	English class
2:00-2:55	Art class
3:00	Go home
3:15-6:00	See my friends in the neighborhood
6:30-7:30	Have dinner
7:30-9:30	Do my homework
9:30-10:00	Get ready for bed

David Byrnes
(352) 222-8542

Vocabulary

Write the correct word or phrase in each blank.

wake up	break	neighborhood	get ready	class

1. I have many friends in my math _____.

2. I like to _____ late on Saturday and Sunday.

3. My best friend lives in my _____.

4. It's time to take a short _____.

Choose the best answer.

1. (   ) At 9:30 a.m., David _____.
    A: wakes up
    B: goes to school
    C: is at home
    D: has a class

2. (   ) In the afternoon, David _____.
    A: has breakfast
    B: does his homework
    C: has three classes
    D: spends time with his friends

3. (   ) How much time does David have to see his friends?
    A: At 3:15.   B: Three hours.
    C: Almost three hours.   D: In the afternoon.

4. (   ) Which of the following is true?
    A: David has six classes a day.
    B: David does his homework before dinner.
    C: English class is after art class.
    D: David's classes last 55 minutes each.

Grammar

Write the correct word in each blank.

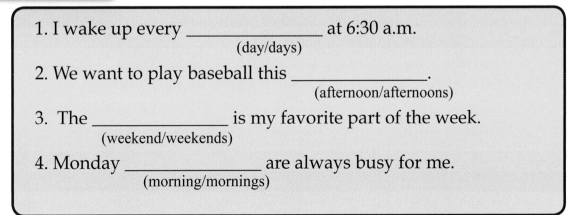

1. I wake up every _____ at 6:30 a.m.
                    (day/days)
2. We want to play baseball this _____.
                              (afternoon/afternoons)
3. The _____ is my favorite part of the week.
        (weekend/weekends)
4. Monday _____ are always busy for me.
          (morning/mornings)

6 Good Hygiene

Good health starts with good hygiene. ___(1)___ a few easy ways to practice good hygiene. Wash your hands ___(2)___ soap often – before eating, after using the restroom, and after going outside. Brush your teeth ___(3)___. And take a shower every day.

Turn these easy activities into good habits. With good hygiene, we keep clean and get sick less. This ___(4)___ diseases from spreading. By doing this, we all stay healthier.

Vocabulary

Write the correct word in each blank.

spread	health	shower	disease	habit

1. Going to sleep late every night is a bad _____.

2. The fire might _____ to other areas.

3. Do you take a _____ in the morning or at night?

4. Exercising can help you stay in good _____.

Reading

Choose the best answer.

1. (　)　A: Have
　　　　　B: Be
　　　　　C: There are
　　　　　D: Can have

2. (　)　A: with
　　　　　B: on
　　　　　C: in
　　　　　D: by

3. (　)　A: one day two times
　　　　　B: two times in the day
　　　　　C: every day twice times
　　　　　D: twice a day

4. (　)　A: helps stop
　　　　　B: to stop
　　　　　C: can stopping
　　　　　D: is stop

Grammar

Write the correct form of each verb.

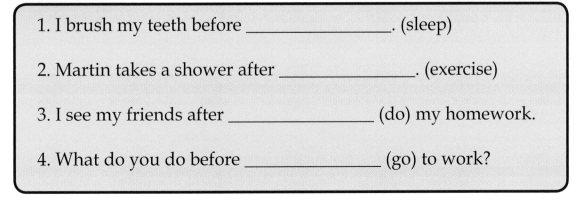

1. I brush my teeth before _____. (sleep)

2. Martin takes a shower after _____. (exercise)

3. I see my friends after _____ (do) my homework.

4. What do you do before _____ (go) to work?

KIRK GIBSON
OUTFIELD

Collecting sports cards is fun. There are cards for many different sports. People like to collect cards of their favorite teams and players.

A pack of cards has between three and ten cards inside, sometimes more. The photographs are great. On most cards, there is information about the athlete. Sometimes companies place special cards inside a pack, such as cards signed by athletes. These items are hard to find. People must buy many packs to find one.

Vocabulary

Write the correct word in each blank.

| information | team | inside | sport | photograph |

1. Who's the best player on your _____?

2. I know a good website with _____ about baseball.

3. Here's a _____ of me in Paris.

4. Let's go _____ . It's raining.

Choose the best answer.

1. (   ) Sports cards _____.
   A: are made for a lot of sports
   B: are all expensive
   C: are hard to collect
   D: come in packs of 10-20 cards

2. (   ) Packs of sports cards _____.
   A: have cards with photographs of athletes on them
   B: usually have a special card like a signed card
   C: have at most three cards inside
   D: cost between three and ten dollars each

3. (   ) What is an "athlete"?
   A: a pack of cards
   B: a special card
   C: a sign
   D: a sports player

4. (   ) Signed cards are _____.
   A: easy to find   B: in every pack
   C: common   D: very rare

Grammar

Complete each sentence with a form of *be*.

1. _____ football your favorite sport?

2. There _____ nine players on a baseball team.

3. _____ I on your team?

4. This _____ not a special card.

8 Lukang

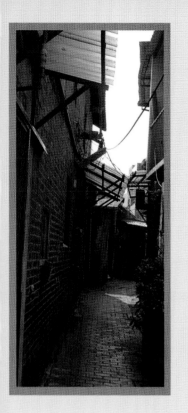

Lukang is an old town in central Taiwan. It has friendly people and interesting things to see. Lukang is famous for narrow streets like Nine Turns Lane. They give people a feeling of walking through history.

Lukang also has delicious snacks. And there are many temples. Tian Hou Gong is the largest. Finally, let's not forget Lukang's big museum with many things from Taiwan's past. A visit to Lukang is a great way to spend a couple of days.

Vocabulary

Write the correct word in each blank.

friendly	temple	narrow	spend	delicious

1. Let's _____ the afternoon at the beach.

2. There is no room for cars on the _____ street.

3. This restaurant has _____ pasta.

4. The people here are very _____.

Choose the best answer.

1. (   ) What is Tian Hou Gong?
        A: A town.
        B: A temple.
        C: A street.
        D: A restaurant.

2. (   ) The article suggests that Nine Turns Lane is _____.
        A: old   B: wide
        C: nine meters long   D: not an interesting thing to see

3. (   ) The article does **not** mention a _____ in Lukang.
        A: street   B: temple
        C: market   D: museum

4. (   ) Which of the following is true?
        A: People can learn about Taiwan's past at Lukang's museum.
        B: It takes weeks to visit Lukang's interesting areas.
        C: Lukang's snacks are more famous than its temples.
        D: The people in Lukang are cold.

Grammar

Put the words in the correct order.

1. museums have the city Does many

_____ ?

2. famous has many temples It

_____ .

3. don't everything We to see have time

_____ .

4. She the city a picture of have doesn't

_____ .

9 Central Springfield

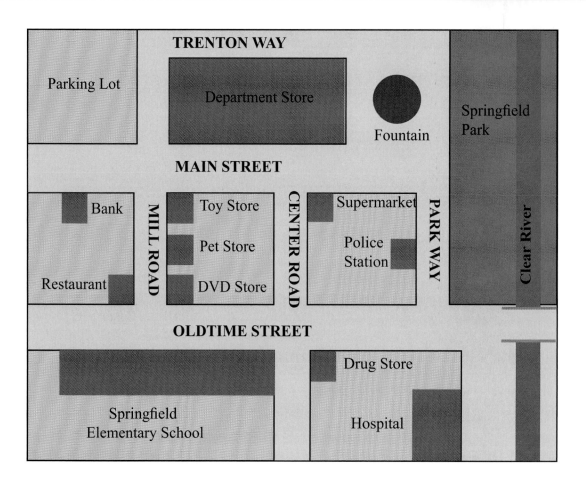

Vocabulary

Write the correct word in each blank.

department store	river	park	supermarket	street

1. In the summer, people swim in the _____.

2. I like to buy clothes at this _____.

3. Janet's house is on the next _____.

4. I bought some apples at the _____.

Choose the best answer.

1. (   ) The pet store is _____.
    A: next to the police station
    B: across the street from the bank
    C: on the corner of Mill Road and Main Street
    D: in between the toy store and DVD store

2. (   ) The drug store is _____ Oldtime Street and Center Road.
    A: on the corner of   B: in between
    C: beside   D: behind

3. (   ) How can you go from the police station to the toy store?
    A: Turn left on Center Road. Then, go down Main Street.
    B: Walk from Park Way to Oldtime Street to Center Road.
    C: Walk all the way up to Trenton Way. Turn right.
    D: Walk up Park Way. Then, turn left on Main Street.

4. (   ) Which of the following is true about central Springfield?
    A: There are many restaurants.
    B: There is a fountain near the park.
    C: There is nowhere to park near the department store.
    D: Most of the stores are on Park Way.

Grammar

Put the words in the correct order.

1. next at Turn street left the

_____ .

2. the here street across from bank The is

_____ .

3. there restaurant here Is a near

_____ ?

10 Plastic Bags

Vocabulary

Write the correct word or phrase in each blank.

total	plastic	appreciate	out of	change

1. I _____ all of your help.

2. Can you tell me the _____ again?

3. These things are _____.

4. We're _____ time.

Choose the best answer.

1. (   ) The cashier _____.
    A: has a lot of change
    B: cannot take the $100 bill from the customer
    C: gives the customer a bag
    D: buys $13.50 worth of items

2. (   ) How does the customer want to pay for his items?
    A: With coins.   B: With a $100 bill.
    C: It's not necessary.   D: The total is $13.50.

3. (   ) Why doesn't the cashier give the customer a bag?
    A: There are no more bags in the store.
    B: The customer doesn't want a bag.
    C: The cashier isn't friendly.
    D: He isn't allowed to.

4. (   ) Which of the following is true?
    A: The customer will carry his items.
    B: The cashier cannot sell anything to the customer.
    C: People cannot sell plastic bags.
    D: The customer doesn't have any money.

Grammar

Put the words in the correct order.

1. give me bag plastic a Will you

_____?

2. his bags will He own bring

_____.

3. him give a bag can't He

_____.

4. change a twenty Can he

_____?

Dolphins live in oceans around the world. There are more than 30 species of these beautiful animals. Some live in small groups of not more than a few. Others live in very large groups of 10,000 or more dolphins. Dolphins use loud squeaking noises to communicate. They can swim very fast – up to 24 miles per hour (40 kilometers).

Dolphins enjoy being with people. They often swim alongside boats. There are even stories of dolphins saving swimmers in trouble.

Vocabulary

Write the correct word in each blank.

group	world	communicate	save	ocean

1. Doctors _____ many lives every day.

2. I use the Internet to _____ with faraway friends.

3. A _____ of rabbits lives near my house.

4. There is no light at the bottom of the _____.

Reading

Choose the best answer.

1. (   ) Dolphin groups _____.
   - A: are always very small
   - B: cannot be larger than 1,000 members
   - C: sometimes include only three or four dolphins
   - D: are mostly very large

2. (   ) How do dolphins communicate?
   - A: By swimming very fast.
   - B: By living in large groups.
   - C: By talking with people.
   - D: By making loud noises.

3. (   ) What is a "member?"
   - A: a species of dolphin
   - B: a part of a group
   - C: a kind of group
   - D: a number or size

4. (   ) Dolphins _____ people.
   - A: sometimes help
   - B: are all afraid of
   - C: stay away from
   - D: are dangerous to

Grammar

Put the words in the correct order.

1. one   group   in   were   There   more   than   100

   _____.

2. live   up   to   They   years   40   can

   _____.

3. usually   live   40   more   than   don't   They   years

   _____.

4. were   more   than   other   in   the   group   There   not   10

   _____.

12 A Hard but Happy Life

Mr. Sanchez works very hard. He wakes up every morning at 6:00 a.m. Then he takes the subway to his office. It's always very busy there. Sometimes he doesn't even have time to eat lunch. The work day ends at around 7:00 p.m.

Mr. Sanchez is happy to go home. He loves eating dinner with his family, talking with his wife, and playing with his children. Spending time with them makes him happy. He's ready for the next long day at work.

Vocabulary

Write the correct word in each blank.

subway	office	dinner	children	family

1. What time should we eat _____ tonight?

2. Mrs. Takara has three _____: two girls and one boy.

3. Ten people work in my _____.

4. Is there a _____ station near your house?

Choose the best answer.

1. (   ) Mr. Sanchez spends _____ at work every day.
    A: from 7 to 7　　　　　　B: less than five hours
    C: 7:00 a.m.　　　　　　　D: more than 10 hours

2. (   ) People at Mr. Sanchez's office _____.
    A: aren't usually busy　　B: have a lot to do
    C: always eat lunch　　　D: go to work at 7:00 p.m.

3. (   ) What words could describe Mr. Sanchez?
    A: Lazy and selfish.
    B: Strange and unkind.
    C: Unhappy and tired.
    D: Hardworking and busy.

4. (   ) Which of the following is true? Mr. Sanchez _____.
    A: often works at home
    B: doesn't have any children
    C: enjoys being with his family
    D: takes the bus

Grammar Use *n't (not)* and change these sentences.

1. He works in the subway station.

    _____.

2. He takes the bus to work.

    _____.

3. He goes home at 6:00.

    _____.

4. He spends time with his friends.

    _____.

13 A Taste of Italy

A Taste of Italy

Bridge of Sighs

Soup

Tomato	$1.50
Vegetable	$2.00

Salad

Large Salad	$3.50
Small Salad	$3.25

Pizza

Cheese	$5.50
Sausage	$7.00
Combo	$8.50

Drinks

Coke	$1.25
Iced Tea	$1.25
Coffee	$1.00

Waiter: Are you ready to order?

Customer: Yes, I want a cheese pizza and a coke.

Waiter: Would you like a soup or salad to go with that?

Customer: OK, a salad sounds good.

Waiter: Then you should get the special. For $8 you can get a pizza, a drink, and soup or a salad.

Customer: That's a good deal. Give me the special, with a salad.

Waiter: Sure thing.

Customer: Thanks very much.

Waiter: You're welcome.

Vocabulary

Write the correct word in each blank.

soup	salad	waiter	customer	deal

1. One hundred dollars for that shirt is a great _____.

2. My sister works as a _____ at a big restaurant.

3. There's not even one _____ in your shop today.

4. Would you like a large _____?

Choose the best answer.

1. (   ) How much do a coke and a combo pizza cost?
      A: $1.25 each.   B: $10.00.
      C: Less than $5.   D: $9.75.

2. (   ) How many kinds of pizza are there?
      A: One.   B: Two.
      C: Three.   D: Four.

3. (   ) The customer does not want _____.
      A: the special
      B: a soup
      C: anything to drink
      D: a pizza

4. (   ) Which of the following is true?
      A: The waiter helps the customer save money.
      B: The restaurant has three kinds of salad.
      C: A bowl of tomato soup is the same price as a coke.
      D: The special comes with a soup, salad, or second pizza.

Grammar

Combine the two sentences into one sentence with *or.*

1. You can have a cheese pizza. You can have a sausage pizza.

    _____

2. You can have a large soup. You can have a small soup.

    _____

3. You can have iced tea. You can have coffee.

    _____

14 Montreal

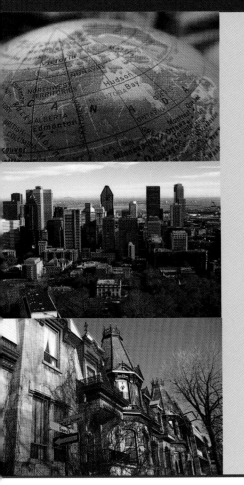

Montreal, a large city in eastern Canada, is rich in history and culture. The city is more than 350 years old. French and English are widely spoken there. That gives the city an international flavor.

Visitors to Montreal like to visit the old churches and streets. They also enjoy the fine museums, like the Museum of Contemporary Art. And there are beautiful parks, like Mount Royal Park. It's on the mountain overlooking the city.

Vocabulary

Write the correct word in each blank.

mountain	enjoy	city	beautiful	history

1. You look _____. Is that a new dress?

2. New York is a crowded and expensive _____.

3. What do you _____ doing in your free time?

4. Most of the trees on this _____ are redwood trees.

Choose the best answer.

1. (   ) Montreal is a(n) _____ city.
   - A: new
   - B: old
   - C: boring
   - D: small

2. (   ) Mount Royal Park looks _____ Montreal.
   - A: down on
   - B: up to
   - C: around
   - D: by

3. (   ) According to the article, what gives Montreal an international flavor?
   - A: Big museums.
   - B: People speaking more than one language.
   - C: Old buildings.
   - D: Beautiful parks.

4. (   ) The article does **not** mention Montreal's _____.
   - A: museums
   - B: location
   - C: businesses
   - D: buildings

Grammar

Match the two parts of the sentence.

1. ___ Montreal is in   A. a fine museum.

2. ___ The city is   B. beautiful parks.

3. ___ There is   C. rich in history.

4. ___ There are   D. eastern Canada.

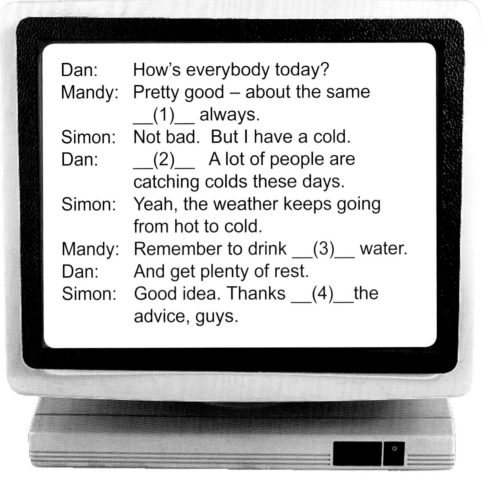

Dan: How's everybody today?
Mandy: Pretty good – about the same __(1)__ always.
Simon: Not bad. But I have a cold.
Dan: __(2)__ A lot of people are catching colds these days.
Simon: Yeah, the weather keeps going from hot to cold.
Mandy: Remember to drink __(3)__ water.
Dan: And get plenty of rest.
Simon: Good idea. Thanks __(4)__ the advice, guys.

Vocabulary

Write the correct word or words in each blank.

catch a cold	remember	plenty of	everybody	advice

1. Can you give me some _____ about finding a job?

2. _____ likes to receive presents.

3. Slow down. We have _____ time.

4. In this cold and wet weather, it's easy to _____.

Choose the best answer.

1. (   )   A: from
           B: when
           C: as
           D: than

2. (   )   A: Lucky you!
           B: Yes, I do.
           C: That's strange.
           D: Sorry to hear that.

3. (   )   A: lot
           B: a lot of
           C: lots
           D: of

4. (   )   A: for
           B: to
           C: at
           D: about

Grammar

Match the two parts of the conversation.

1. ___ How are you?   **A.** I will, thanks.

2. ___ What's the matter?   **B.** I have a cold.

3. ___ That's too bad.   **C.** Not so good.

4. ___ Well, take care of yourself.   **D.** Yeah, I can't go out.

16 Making a Bean Taco

1. To make a taco, you can use hard or soft taco shells. You also need lettuce, tomatoes, cheese, and refried beans.

2. First, cut the tomatoes, lettuce, and cheese into small pieces. Then, heat the beans.

3. Next, put some beans into a shell. Then, add some lettuce and tomatoes. After that, add cheese. You can also add a sauce.

4. Your taco is ready! Tacos are often served with rice, salad, and beans. It's a simple meal. But it can fill you up!

Vocabulary

Write the correct word in each blank.

cut	piece	ready	need	meal

1. Breakfast is the first _____ of the day.

2. Would you like a _____ of cake?

3. I _____ some help lifting this table.

4. The bus is coming soon. Get _____ to leave.

Choose the best answer.

1. (   ) What does the reading say about tacos?
   - A: They're filled with beans, tomatoes, lettuce, and cheese.
   - B: They take a long time to prepare.
   - C: They must be served with salad.
   - D: They taste better with hard shells.

2. (   ) The _____ should be cut into little pieces.
   - A: beans
   - B: taco shell
   - C: sauce
   - D: tomatoes

3. (   ) Which of these actions comes first?
   - A: Adding sauce to the taco.
   - B: Heating the beans.
   - C: Putting the beans into the shell.
   - D: Adding cheese to the taco.

4. (   ) Which of these is **not** needed to make a bean taco?
   - A: A taco shell.
   - B: Rice.
   - C: Cheese.
   - D: Beans.

Grammar

Fill in each blank with *next, first, finally,* or *second.*

Making a salad is pretty easy. _____, get all the vegetables together. _____, wash them well. _____, cut up the lettuce and tomatoes. _____, mix everything together in a bowl.

17 Gift Shop

Regalos ✵ Gifts
2333 Blossom Hill Road
San Jose, CA 95030

Date: July 23, 2009
Time: 8:54 p.m.

Item	Quantity	Price
Black Sony telephone	1	$37.50
Box of candy	1	$7.50
Roll of film	2	$4.00
DVD - The Lion King	1	$15.00
Roll of gift wrap	1	$3.00
Subtotal		$67.00
Tax (5%)		$3.35
Total		$70.35

Vocabulary

Write the correct word in each blank.

telephone	time	roll of film	tax	each

1. This _____ has pictures of our trip to Japan.

2. What _____ does the store open?

3. These shirts cost $30, and the _____ is $1.50.

4. You can use my _____ to call your mother.

34

Reading

Choose the best answer.

1. (　) The receipt is from _____.
　　　　A: a morning sale
　　　　B: a month in spring
　　　　C: a store in San Jose
　　　　D: a store on Gift Palace Road

2. (　) How many items does the customer buy?
　　　　A: One.　　　　　B: Five.
　　　　C: Six.　　　　　D: About 70.

3. (　) What is the most expensive item?
　　　　A: The roll of film.　　　B: The telephone.
　　　　C: The DVD.　　　　　D: The picture frame.

4. (　) Let's say the customer wants another roll of gift wrap.
　　　　How much more does he pay?
　　　　A: $0.15
　　　　B: $3.00
　　　　C: $3.15
　　　　D: $70.35

Grammar

Write the correct word or words in each blank.

1. I need two _____, please.
　　(roll of wraps/rolls of wrap)

2. She wants to buy _____.
　　　　(gift/gifts)

3. These are all great _____!
　　　　(DVDs/DVD)

4. They have many _____.
　　　(boxes of candy/box of candies)

18 Clubs

There are all kinds of clubs for people of all ages. Some are for music lovers. Others are for hiking. There are even clubs for making art. People with similar interests join clubs. It's a good way to meet people.

To get new members, clubs have special activities. They make big posters. They also hold parties. Club members tell other people about the club. They display photos, pictures, and examples of what the club does.

Tonight

CHESS CLUB

Locksley Hall 213

HIKING · CAMPING · MOUNTAIN CLIMBING
Organizing meeting FSU Outing Club 9/15 7 p.m. Student Union G

Vocabulary

Write the correct word in each blank.

similar	display	activities	members	age

1. All of our club _____ love singing.

2. I have a jacket _____ to this one.

3. I love the way these stores _____ their products.

4. It's cold in the winter. Most of our _____ are indoors.

Choose the best answer.

1. ( ) Clubs are nice for _____.
   A: young people only
   B: meeting people
   C: universities but not other schools
   D: people with very different interests

2. ( ) The reading does **not** mention clubs for _____.
   A: computers   B: hiking
   C: music   D: art

3. ( ) What does "of all ages" mean?
   A: very old   B: young and old
   C: about 25 years old   D: at a certain age

4. ( ) How do clubs attract new members?
   A: They send them photos.
   B: They hold activities.
   C: They give them money.
   D: They sell posters.

Grammar

Put the words in the correct order.

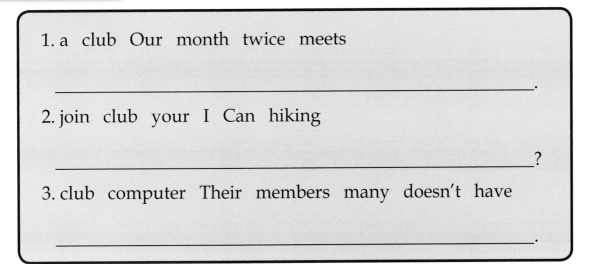

1. a club Our month twice meets

   _____.

2. join club your I Can hiking

   _____?

3. club computer Their members many doesn't have

   _____.

19 Ramadan

Ramadan is an important Muslim celebration. It lasts one month. During each day of Ramadan, Muslims fast all day – between dawn and sunset. So people eat before dawn. After sunset, people enjoy meals with friends and relatives.

During the fast, people should not lie or have bad thoughts. Ramadan is a time to pray a lot, think about life, and become a better person. After the last day of Ramadan, there is a big holiday. People visit each other and have special meals.

Vocabulary

Write the correct word in each blank.

relatives	pray	sunset	lie	dawn

1. My grandfather is a farmer. He wakes up before _____.

2. Many of my _____ live in Canada.

3. It's wrong to _____ to people.

4. Every week, we go to a mosque to _____.

Choose the best answer.

1. (   ) Ramadan lasts _____.
   A: all year   B: about 30 days
   C: one night   D: from sunset to dawn

2. (   ) During Ramadan, Muslims do not eat _____.
   A: during the day   B: at night
   C: before dawn   D: after sunset

3. (   ) What is something a person should not do during Ramadan?
   A: Visit friends.
   B: Pray and think about life.
   C: Speak untrue words.
   D: Have good thoughts.

4. (   ) What happens when Ramadan ends?
   A: People fast for one month.
   B: Muslims stop visiting friends.
   C: People eat too much.
   D: There are big parties.

Grammar

Complete each sentence with *during* or *after*.

1. _____ Ramadan Muslims fast all day.

2. _____ sunset they break their fast.

3. _____ the day people pray a lot.

4. _____ Ramadan there is a holiday.

20 Learning English

Franz: What's your favorite class?
Mine's math.

Tina: English, for sure.

Franz: Really? Why?

Tina: It's fun to speak a second language. I feel like a different person.

Franz: That's interesting. But what about the homework? It's so hard!

Tina: Every class has homework, right?

Franz: That's true. Hey, do you want to study together for next week's test?

Tina: Sure. Two heads are better than one.

Vocabulary

Write the correct word in each blank.

favorite	hard	interesting	different	next

1. Do you want to try this shirt on – or maybe a _____ one?

2. This book is really _____. You should read it.

3. What's your _____ kind of music?

4. Mr. Johnson's tests are so _____. I have to study for hours before each of them.

Choose the best answer.

1. (   ) Learning English is _____ for Tina.
     A: too hard   B: interesting
     C: wrong   D: not fun

2. (   ) Franz is worried about the _____ in English class.
     A: homework   B: students
     C: math   D: teachers

3. (   ) What does "Two heads are better than one" mean?
     A: People with two heads are smart.
     B: Working together is a good idea.
     C: One person should never work alone.
     D: Working is hard for everyone.

4. (   ) Which of the following is true?
     A: Tina doesn't do her homework.
     B: English is Franz's favorite class.
     C: Tina and Franz have different favorite classes.
     D: Tina and Franz can't study together.

Grammar

Match the correct sentences.

1. ___ That is yours and mine.   **A.** It's hers.

2. ___ That is Roberto's.   **B.** It's theirs.

3. ___ That is Roberto's and Maria's.   **C.** It's ours.

4. ___ That is Maria's.   **D.** It's his.

21 Apartments for Rent

A. Lovely little apartment in new building. One bedroom, one bathroom, living room. Furnished. $750 per month.

B. Large downtown apartment. One minute walk to subway. Three bedrooms (two large, one small), large bathroom, BIG kitchen. Partly furnished. $1,200 per month.

C. Studio for rent. Great for student or busy working person. $350 per month.

D. Two-story apartment in the new, private Lakewoods Heights. Swimming pool, exercise room, full-time guard. Large play area for kids. $1,500 per month.

Vocabulary

Write the correct word in each blank.

| building | private | living room | full-time | kitchen |

1. I work _____ as a painter.

2. Wow, you live in such a tall _____.

3. It's nice to cook in a big _____.

4. I want to buy a new sofa for my _____.

Choose the best answer.

1. (　) Apartment A _____.
   A: is smaller than Apartment D
   B: probably doesn't have any tables or chairs
   C: is very big
   D: is less than $350 per month

2. (　) What do we know about Apartment B?
   A: It's in the countryside.
   B: It's far from the center of the city.
   C: The kitchen is very small.
   D: It has two large bedrooms.

3. (　) Jack and Nancy have children. They're looking for a safe
   building. Which apartment is best for them?
   A: Apartment A.   B: Apartment B.
   C: Apartment C.   D: Apartment D.

4. (　) Maria doesn't spend much time at home. She works a lot.
   She wants a small place. Which apartment is best for her?
   A: Apartment A.   B: Apartment B.
   C: Apartment C.   D: Apartment D.

Grammar　Use *not* and change these sentences.

1. We live in a three-story apartment.

   _____

2. It has a fully-furnished living room.

   _____

3. It has a very large kitchen.

   _____

22 Jackie Chan

Jackie Chan is an international superstar. His movies are full of action. They're also very funny. They're never boring. In the action scenes, people throw strange things like tables and chairs. Jackie does all those scenes himself. It can be a little dangerous. In fact, Jackie sometimes gets hurt.

Jackie makes movies in Asia and America. He often stars with other famous actors. They enjoy working with him. Jackie Chan's movies are really fun.

Vocabulary

Write the correct word in each blank.

dangerous	hurt	international	strange	action

1. IBM is a famous _____ company.

2. Working as a policeman can be _____.

3. Many people are _____ in car accidents every year.

4. _____ movies are very exciting.

Choose the best answer.

1. (   ) Which words could describe Jackie Chan?
       A: Brave and funny.
       B: Afraid and boring.
       C: Shy and quiet.
       D: Serious and calm.

2. (   ) What's an example of a strange item in an action scene?
       A: A gun.   B: A knife.
       C: A stick.   D: An egg.

3. (   ) Why is Jackie sometimes hurt?
       A: His action scenes aren't always safe.
       B: He only fights in Asia and America.
       C: He doesn't like other famous actors.
       D: Many people want to hurt him.

4. (   ) Which of the following is **not** true?
       A: Jackie works in more than one country.
       B: Jackie is not the only star in his movies.
       C: Jackie is only popular in Asia.
       D: Jackie's movies make people laugh.

Grammar

Complete each sentence with *never, sometimes* or *often*.

1. I really love the movies. I _____ go with my friends.

2. Pete doesn't go very often, but he _____ sees a Jackie Chan movie.

3. Lee only watches DVDs. He_____ goes to a movie theater.

4. I love popcorn, so I _____ buy it.

23 Email

From: n.ruby@freemail.com (Neil Ruby)

To: rocketman@aol.com (Jeff Taylor)

Subject: Hot summer

Hey Jeff,

How's it going? Are you enjoying the summer? The weather here is HOT! I don't even like going outside. Sometimes I go outside – to go swimming!

Do you remember my dog Pango? Well, now she's a mother, with five puppies. They're cute. Do you want one?

Let's see… Oh, my sister is going to university soon. That's pretty cool. Then, I can have her room. Yes!

Keep in touch,

Neil

Vocabulary

Write the correct word in each blank.

| summer | puppy | weather | swimming | sometimes |

1. I like to go _____.

2. _____, I spend several hours playing computer games.

3. The _____ should get cooler later today.

4. How old is your _____?

Choose the best answer.

1. (   ) Neil _____ hot weather.
    A: loves   B: prefers
    C: doesn't mind   D: doesn't like

2. (   ) What do we learn about the puppies?
    A: Neil wants to give away at least one of them.
    B: There are six of them.
    C: Neil is keeping them all.
    D: Jeff doesn't like them.

3. (   ) What does "Keep in touch" mean?
    A: Be well.
    B: Stay in contact.
    C: Take care.
    D: Enjoy yourself.

4. (   ) Which of the following is true?
    A: Neil offers Jeff a puppy.
    B: Neil never goes outside.
    C: Jeff's area is very hot.
    D: Jeff doesn't know Pango.

Grammar

Put the words in the correct order.

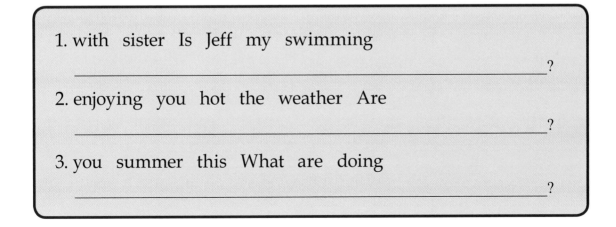

1. with   sister   Is   Jeff   my   swimming
    _____?

2. enjoying   you   hot   the   weather   Are
    _____?

3. you   summer   this   What   are   doing
    _____?

24 Howard in a Hurry

Howard is always in a hurry. He walks very ___(1)___. He eats fast food for lunch and dinner. He even speaks fast – more than 100 words ___(2)___ minute.

Howard doesn't like to wait in lines. He always pushes his way to the front. Howard has to be the first person ___(3)___ a bus. His friends tell him to slow down. But ___(4)___. Do you know anybody like Howard?

Vocabulary

Write the correct word in each blank.

push	line	slow down	fast	anybody

1. You're speaking too _____. I don't understand.

2. Does _____ know Tom's phone number?

3. The _____ for this movie is too long!

4. _____. You don't need to work so fast.

Choose the best answer.

1. (   )   A: slowly
B: fast
C: carefully
D: fully

2. (   )   A: in
B: the
C: per
D: at

3. (   )   A: in and out
B: on and off
C: up and down
D: to and from

4. (   )   A: that's hard for him to do
B: he's hard to do that
C: it's so hard to him
D: he is too hard

Grammar

Put the words in the correct order.

1. does walk How he fast

_____?

2. long wait he How does

_____?

3. fast does How he speak

_____?

3. he How can go far

_____?

49

25 Clothes Shopping

Vocabulary

Write the correct word in each blank.

budget	kind of	price	silk	tie

1. The _____ of the ring is 5,000 dollars.

2. We can't spend more than our _____.

3. A blue _____ would go well with that shirt.

4. It's _____ hot in here.

Choose the best answer.

1. (   ) The man is shopping for _____.
   A: himself   B: a shirt
   C: an expensive present   D: his father

2. (   ) What does the man think about the first group of ties?
   A: He loves them.
   B: He hates them.
   C: He asks his father about them.
   D: He doesn't like the price.

3. (   ) The store _____.
   A: doesn't carry ties from Italy
   B: has many ties to choose from
   C: has only one color of tie
   D: only sells expensive ties

4. (   ) To the shopper, the _____ of the item is important.
   A: price   B: brand
   C: material   D: popularity

Grammar

Match each question with the correct answer.

1. __ Can I help you?   **A.** It's too expensive.

2. __ What are you looking for?   **B.** I'm just looking, thanks.

3. __ How do you like this one?   **C.** Large, I guess.

4. __ What's your size?   **D.** A new coat.

26 Shinkansen

The Shinkansen (also called "bullet train") is Japan's super fast train. It can travel 270 kilometers per hour. Bullet trains are fast, comfortable, and quiet. They are also very expensive. Tickets cost much more than tickets for local trains.

Ticket prices		
	Local	Shinkansen
Tokyo to Nagoya	6,000 yen	10,000 yen
Tokyo to Kyoto	7,800 yen	13,000 yen
Tokyo to Osaka	8,300 yen	13,500 yen

Vocabulary

Write the correct word in each blank.

kilometer	ticket	expensive	comfortable	travel

1. How much is a _____ to Tokyo?

2. I can't buy it. It's too _____.

3. I love your sofa. It's so _____.

4. I want to _____ to Korea one day.

Choose the best answer.

1. (   ) Bullet trains _____.
   A: don't cost very much
   B: only go from Tokyo to Osaka
   C: are noisy
   D: cost more than local trains

2. (   ) What's good about local trains?
   A: They are not too expensive.   B: They are fast.
   C: They cost a lot.   D: They are loud.

3. (   ) A ticket from Tokyo to Osaka on a local train costs _____
   _____.
   A: 6,000 yen   B: 8,300 yen
   C: 13,000 yen   D: 13,500 yen

4. (   ) Which of the following is true?
   A: There is no Shinkansen from Tokyo to Kyoto.
   B: The Shinkansen is faster than a bullet.
   C: The Shinkansen can travel 270 miles per hour.
   D: The local train from Tokyo to Kyoto costs less than
       8,000 yen.

Grammar

Write the correct word in each blank.

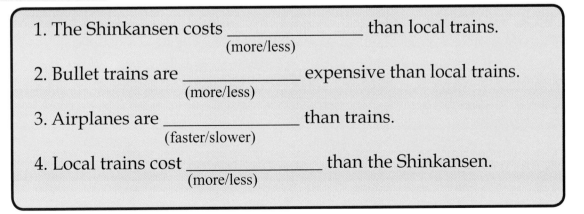

1. The Shinkansen costs _____ than local trains.
   (more/less)

2. Bullet trains are _____ expensive than local trains.
   (more/less)

3. Airplanes are _____ than trains.
   (faster/slower)

4. Local trains cost _____ than the Shinkansen.
   (more/less)

27 Making Rain

People use a lot of water – for cooking, washing, drinking, and so on. Rain is the main source of new water. Unfortunately, it doesn't always rain enough. That can be a big problem.

Sometimes we can help make rain. To do this, a special airplane flies up to the clouds. Then it releases some chemicals. These chemicals cause clouds to make rain. This is called "seeding clouds." Seeding clouds can help bring water to thirsty cities and towns.

Vocabulary

Write the correct word in each blank.

thirsty	fly	unfortunately	chemical	cause

1. Typhoons _____ problems for people and cities.

2. Give the _____ baby something to drink.

3. _____, I can't go with you to the mall.

4. Many birds _____ south in the winter.

Choose the best answer.

1. (   ) Where does a lot of water for cities come from?
   A: Rivers.   B: Lakes.
   C: Rain.   D: Mountains.

2. (   ) According to the article, without enough rain _____.
   A: people do a lot of cooking
   B: people use more water
   C: cities look for other sources of water
   D: cities have problems

3. (   ) What is "seeding clouds"?
   A: a kind of cloud   B: a way to make rain
   C: a chemical   D: a special airplane

4. (   ) What happens first?
   A: Special airplanes let out chemicals.
   B: An airplane flies up high in the sky.
   C: Cloud seeding causes clouds to make rain.
   D: It rains a lot.

Grammar

Complete each sentence with *do, does, doesn't,* or *don't.*

1. Do you drink soda? No, I _____.

2. Doesn't it rain here in July? No, it _____.

3. Does she like to fly? No, she _____.

4. Do they use a lot of water? Yes, they _____.

28 Short Message

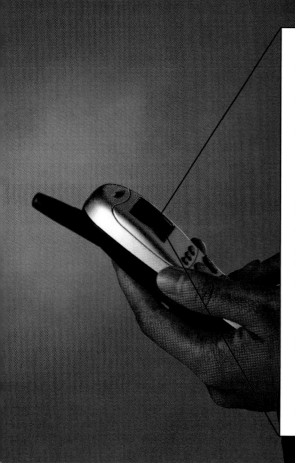

Hi, Donna. It's Jack. I have some bad news. I have to cancel our dinner date. I need to stay at work and finish a few things.

I'm really sorry. Please don't be mad at me! Maybe we can have dinner one day next week. Are you free on Wednesday? Give me a call and let me know.

My boss is coming. I better get back to work. Talk to you soon.

Jack

Vocabulary

Write the correct word in each blank.

boss	date	finish	cancel	mad

1. Please _____ your homework before 9:00 PM.

2. I have a _____ with Jennifer this Saturday.

3. We have a new _____ at our company.

4. You have too many credit cards. You should _____ one of them.

Reading

Choose the best answer.

1. (　) Why does Jack cancel the date?
        A: He doesn't like Donna.
        B: He has to work late.
        C: He doesn't have a reason.
        D: He has to meet with his boss.

2. (　) Jack feels _____ about canceling the date.
        A: fine   B: happy
        C: bad   D: mad

3. (　) Jack wants to _____.
        A: see Donna next week
        B: call Donna another time
        C: have dinner with his boss
        D: work late on Wednesday

4. (　) What does "let me know" mean?
        A: tell me
        B: give it to me
        C: let me do it
        D: I know you

Grammar

Put the words in the correct order.

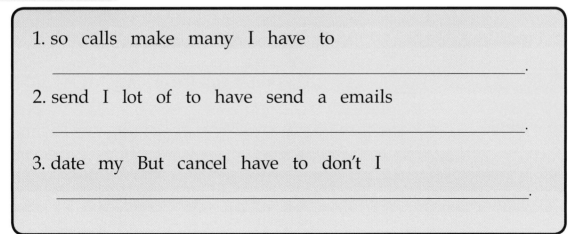

1. so calls make many I have to

_____.

2. send I lot of to have send a emails

_____.

3. date my But cancel have to don't I

_____.

You're invited to a party! Join us for food, fun, and a crazy time to celebrate:

the 50th birthday of Richard Marley
on Friday, July 13th
from 2:00-9:00 p.m.
at Golden Sun Park

Remember to bring your swimsuit and dancing shoes. Call or email us for directions to the park or t o arrange a ride.

Tel: (605) 392-4814
Email: smarley@yahoo.com

Vocabulary

Write the correct word in each blank.

birthday	invite	directions	celebrate	arrange

1. Can you give me _____ to your house?

2. I want to _____ 10 or 15 people to the party.

3. Is your _____ in April or May?

4. People like to _____ holidays with their families.

Choose the best answer.

1. (　) People can _____ at the party.
   A: swim
   B: make a cake
   C: ask for directions
   D: buy a swimsuit

2. (　) People without a car _____ to the party.
   A: can ask for a ride
   B: can't go
   C: have to take a taxi
   D: can arrange a bus

3. (　) The invitation does **not** include _____.
   A: an email address　　　B: a time and date
   C: directions　　　　　　D: a telephone number

4. (　) Which of the following is true?
   A: The party starts at three.
   B: Richard's birthday is in the winter.
   C: The party should last seven hours.
   D: Richard is 30 years old.

Grammar

Complete each sentence with *to* or *for*.

1. The present is _____ my friend.

2. You can give it _____ her at the party.

3. Please call _____ directions _____ the park.

4. Can I ask you _____ a ride?

30 Weekend Plans

Lupita: What are your plans for the weekend?

Anders: I'm not sure. I might go to a movie.

Lupita: Cool, which one?

Anders: I don't know. I need to check the newspaper. So, do you have any plans?

Lupita: Nothing fun. I need to help my dad at his store. But that's just on Saturday until five or so.

Anders: Well, how about after that? We can get something to eat and see a movie.

Lupita: Sounds good. Let's talk about it again this Friday.

Vocabulary

Write the correct word in each blank.

newspaper	check	movie	plans	help

1. It might be raining. Go and _____ outside.

2. Do you have any _____ for the winter holiday?

3. I like to read the _____ every Sunday morning.

4. Can you _____ me fix my computer?

Choose the best answer.

1. (   ) What movie does Anders want to see?
   A: He's not sure.
   B: The one with Lupita in it.
   C: Something about Lupita's dad.
   D: Nothing fun.

2. (   ) On Saturday, Lupita needs to _____.
   A: find a job   B: help a parent
   C: read a newspaper   D: cook something

3. (   ) What does "Sounds good" mean?
   A: No way.   B: I can hear it.
   C: The voice is nice. D: It's a good idea.

4. (   ) Which of the following is true?
   A: Lupita never has any fun.
   B: There are no interesting movies to watch.
   C: Lupita's dad doesn't need help at his store.
   D: Anders wants to have a meal and see a movie.

Grammar

Put the words in the correct order.

1. plans to make need to We some

   _____.

2. After five don't I to work need

   _____.

3. the paper check you to Do need

   _____?

31 Mexico City

Mexico City is the capital of Mexico. It's the home of more than 21 million people. Mexico City is the heart of Mexico's economy. Most Mexican and foreign businesses have their main offices in the city.

Mexico City is an interesting place to visit. There are large parks, palaces, museums, and monuments. Near the city there are beautiful natural places like forests, mountains, and volcanoes. All in all, it's a great city to visit.

Vocabulary

Write the correct word in each blank.

million	foreign	economy	capital	natural

1. Tokyo is Japan's _____.

2. Repairs to the hotel will cost several _____ dollars.

3. Flowers are a nice way to bring _____ things into your home.

4. Learning a _____ language takes time.

Reading

Choose the best answer.

1. (   ) Why do many businesses open their main
offices in Mexico City?
    A: The city is cheap.
    B: Mexico City is very important to Mexico's economy.
    C: There are a lot of people in the city.
    D: The city has many interesting things to see.

2. (   ) The article does **not** mention Mexico City's _____.
    A: palaces   B: museums
    C: movie theaters   D: parks

3. (   ) What does "all in all" mean?
    A: inside everything   B: considering all things
    C: partly   D: all the problems

4. (   ) About _____ people live in Mexico City.
    A: 20
    B: 2,100
    C: 210,000
    D: 21,000,000

Grammar

Put the words in the correct order.

1. capital   Mexico City   is   of   the   Mexico

    _____.

2. heart   economy   also   Is   the   Mexico   of   City   the

    _____?

3. city   The   is   home   of   the   many   people

    _____.

32 Website

Fastnews.com

Main sections:

Nation
World
Business
Sports
Entertainment

Other

Free e-Chatroom
Forum

"Red" is a hero.

Top Stories

Nation
Pet dog saves man's life

World
America's new leader

Business
Sony's profits are up

Sports
NBA stars get ready for All Star game

Entertainment
Tom Cruise's hot new movie

Website search:

[ ] Go

Internet search:

[ ] Go

Advertisement:

Jake's Pizza Order on-line!

Vocabulary

Write the correct word in each blank.

| Internet | website | search | email | chatroom |

1. I like to talk with my friends in a _____.

2. Yahoo is my favorite _____.

3. The _____ is the home of millions of websites.

4. I need to _____ for information about Russia.

Choose the best answer.

1. (   ) The website has _____.
      A: five main sections
      B: only three sections about news
      C: a special section about dogs
      D: an advertisement search box

2. (   ) What can visitors to the site do?
      A: Write news stories.
      B: Talk with other people.
      C: Get free pizza.
      D: Learn everything about dogs.

3. (   ) Fastnews.com does **not** offer free _____.
      A: forums   B: news stories
      C: chatrooms   D: Internet accounts

4. (   ) The advertisement _____.
      A: is at the top of the page
      B: is in the center of the page
      C: is on one side of the page
      D: is next to the picture of the dog

Grammar

Complete each sentence with *in, on,* or *from.*

1. I learn a lot _____ my friends.

2. There's so much information _____ the Internet.

3. It's fun to talk to people _____ chatrooms.

4. Peter says a lot of funny things _____ his emails.

33 Volunteering

Anyone can be a volunteer. It doesn't matter how old you are. And it's a great way to help others.

There are many ways to volunteer. You can help at a library or school, or you can spend time with old people. You can also help clean your neighborhood's streets and parks.

There is usually a big need for volunteers. It only takes a little bit of time each week. In return, you receive many big smiles and thanks.

Vocabulary

Write the correct word in each blank.

smile	way	usually	receive	library

1. What time do you _____ wake up?

2. It takes me 10 minutes to walk from my house to my _____.

3. Your mother has such a beautiful _____!

4. Practicing often is a good _____ to become a better English speaker.

Reading

Choose the best answer.

1. (   ) Volunteers _____.
   A: are always adults   B: may be any age
   C: usually help at libraries D: are not often needed

2. (   ) What payment do volunteers get?
   A: A lot of money.
   B: The thanks of other people.
   C: Food and other things.
   D: Some money, but not much.

3. (   ) What does "it doesn't matter" mean?
   A: it's not necessary
   B: it's not right
   C: it's not possible
   D: it's not important

4. (   ) The article does **not** mention what type of volunteering?
   A: Cleaning one's neighborhood.
   B: Keeping old people company.
   C: Reading books to young people.
   D: Spending time at a school.

Grammar

Complete each sentence with *much* or *many*.

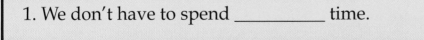

1. We don't have to spend _____ time.

2. _____ students are helping clean the beach.

3. How _____ volunteers do we need?

4. How _____ help can you give?

Every new thing slowly becomes old. Very old things (at least 20 years old) __(1)__ antiques. Anything can be an antique: cars, books, tables, __(2)__. Many people like to buy antiques. They give people a special feeling.

Some antiques are very valuable. People collect them and __(3)__ them. They put them in their homes and offices. Museums __(4)__ very old antiques. That way, everybody can enjoy them. Antiques help us learn about our past.

Vocabulary

Write the correct word in each blank.

learn	become	valuable	feeling	museum

1. Of course the ring is _____. It's made of gold.

2. I want to _____ more about airplanes.

3. This old house gives me a strange _____.

4. Do you want to go to the art _____ with me?

Choose the best answer.

1. ( ) A: are
           B: call
           C: be
           D: they are

2. ( ) A: such as
           B: to example
           C: more
           D: and so on

3. ( ) A: care
           B: very well care
           C: take good care of
           D: caring so good

4. ( ) A: they show
           B: show
           C: showing
           D: shows

Put the words in the correct order.

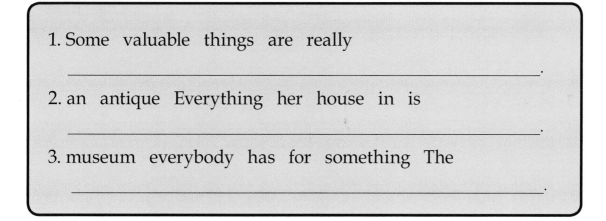

1. Some valuable things are really

   _____.

2. an antique Everything her house in is

   _____.

3. museum everybody has for something The

   _____.

35 Helping at the Family Business

Abdul's family owns a restaurant called Mideast Feast. His mother and father work there every day. Several days a week (after school and on weekends), Abdul goes to the restaurant. He does his homework in the back room.

Sometimes the restaurant is full of people. Abdul's mother and father need his help. He cleans tables and brings water to customers. Abdul also helps in the kitchen. He really likes that. He can taste many kinds of food.

Vocabulary

Write the correct word in each blank.

homework	taste	weekend	restaurant	own

1. There's a great French _____ near my house.

2. I want to _____ a big car one day.

3. Here, _____ some of this soup.

4. What do you like to do on the _____?

Choose the best answer.

1. (   ) Abdul is a _____ son.
      A: lazy   B: terrible
      C: helpful   D: full

2. (   ) How often does Abdul go to the restaurant?
      A: Many times a week.
      B: Every day.
      C: On Saturday and Sunday only.
      D: Very rarely.

3. (   ) Abdul does **not** _____.
      A: help in the kitchen
      B: clean tables
      C: bring people water
      D: take people's orders

4. (   ) Which of the following is true?
      A: Abdul doesn't do his homework.
      B: Abdul's parents bring him to the restaurant.
      C: The restaurant is almost never busy.
      D: Working in the kitchen is fun for Abdul.

Grammar

Combine the two sentences into one with *and*.

1. He goes to the restaurant. He does his homework there.

_____.

2. Does he clean the tables? Does he help in the kitchen?

_____.

3. He goes there after school. He goes on weekends.

_____.

36 Telephone Message

Curt: Hello?

Mandy: Hi, Curt. Is Fred there?

Curt: Sorry, he's not.

Mandy: Oh, no. I really need to talk to him.

Curt: Can I take a message?

Mandy: Yes, please. Tell him to call me. It's urgent.

Curt: No problem, Mandy. Does he have your number?

Mandy: He should. But let me give it to you. It's 489-3583.

Curt: OK, got it.

Mandy: Thanks very much.

Curt: You're welcome.

Vocabulary

Write the correct word in each blank.

really	urgent	message	sorry	problem

1. I'm _____ I broke your glasses.

2. Several unhappy workers have a big _____ with their boss.

3. Remember to write the _____ down and put it near the telephone.

4. I need it now. It's _____.

Reading

Choose the best answer.

1. ( ) The caller is looking for _____.
    A: Mandy   B: Curt
    C: Fred   D: urgent

2. ( ) Curt offers to _____.
    A: give Mandy Fred's cell phone number
    B: pass on a message to Fred
    C: give Mandy a message
    D: call Mandy back

3. ( ) What does "It's urgent" mean?
    A: That doesn't matter.
    B: It's a small problem.
    C: There's no hurry.
    D: It's very important.

4. ( ) Curt is _____ to Mandy.
    A: polite   B: strange
    C: unfriendly   D: rude

Grammar

Match each question with the correct answer.

1. __ Where is Jane?   **A.** Sure, what is it?

2. __ Can I leave a message?   **B.** No, he's not.

3. __ Is Mr. Lee there?   **C.** I'm sorry, I can't.

4. __ Can you give me his cell   **D.** At the office.
    phone number?

37 Siestas

In the south of Spain, siestas are an important part of the local culture. A siesta is a period of rest. During the siesta, from around 1:30 to 4:30 p.m., many businesses close their doors. People go home to rest or eat. Then they go back to work.

The weather in the south of Spain can get very hot. Siestas are a way to get away from the heat. Not every business follows this old custom. But many still do.

Vocabulary

Write the correct word in each blank.

culture	during	custom	business	period

1. What do you usually do _____ your afternoon break?

2. My brother's dream is to open his own _____.

3. The Chinese _____ of eating with chopsticks is very old.

4. Understanding a country's _____ helps us understand its people.

Reading

Choose the best answer.

1. (   ) During siestas, people _____.
       A: work hard
       B: open their businesses
       C: take a rest at home
       D: go to church

2. (   ) How long do siestas last?
       A: About three hours.   B: In the afternoon.
       C: At 1:30.   D: Until 4:30 p.m.

3. (   ) Why do people take siestas?
       A: They work too hard during the day.
       B: They need to work at home.
       C: To follow the custom of all the other businesses.
       D: To get away from the hot weather.

4. (   ) Which of the following is **not** true?
       A: People in some businesses do not take siestas.
       B: Siestas are common in every part of Spain.
       C: Siestas take place in the afternoon.
       D: The custom of taking siestas is not new.

Grammar

Put the words in the correct order.

1. Spain   all   of   Not   custom   follows   this

    _____.

2. business   Not   closes   every   doors   its

    _____.

3. a   people   siesta   many   Not   take

    _____.

38 Child Prodigies

Child prodigies are very special children. At a young age (maybe only 2 or 3 years old), they become very good at certain things. They learn quickly, often without trying hard.

There are child prodigies in many areas, like music, math, sports, and art. Two famous examples are Mozart in music and Tiger Woods in golf.

Life isn't always easy for these special children. People want them to do great things, so people often put a lot of pressure on them.

Write the correct word in each blank.

famous	life	special	pressure	young

1. Michael Jordan is a _____ person. Almost everyone knows his face.

2. The little boy can't go into the bar. He's too _____.

3. My grandmother enjoys her slow and peaceful _____.

4. Students often feel _____ before a big test.

76

Reading

Choose the best answer.

1. (   ) How could we describe child prodigies?
   A: Smart but pressured.
   B: Lazy but special.
   C: Normal but important.
   D: Strange but dangerous.

2. (   ) What trouble do child prodigies have?
   A: They have a lot of work to do.
   B: People give them a lot of pressure.
   C: They don't like being smart.
   D: The world doesn't want them.

3. (   ) Why does the reading mention Tiger Woods?
   A: To teach us about golf.
   B: To show how he is different from Mozart.
   C: To tell us about a normal boy.
   D: To give an example of a child prodigy.

4. (   ) In the final sentence, who or what are "them?"
   A: adults   B: special skills
   C: great things   D: child prodigies

Grammar

Match the two parts of the sentence.

1. ___ Tiger Woods became   **A.** music at the age of 5.

2. ___ Picasso painted   **B.** a play at 12.

3. ___ Lope de Vega wrote   **C.** a golfer at age 3.

4. ___ Mozart composed   **D.** his first picture at 8.

39 Traveling to Guadalajara

Average Rainfall in Guadalajara

Jill and Steven are planning a trip to Guadalajara, Mexico. They prefer dry weather. Also, they don't like traveling in winter. Steven cannot travel in October. He has important work to do at home.

Vocabulary

Write the correct word in each blank.

prefer	average	important	amount	plan

1. The _____ price of houses in this area is very high.

2. Come here. I've got something _____ to tell you.

3. Do you _____ living in the city or countryside?

4. I _____ to be here all day, so you can call me anytime.

Choose the best answer.

1. (   ) What month gets the most rainfall in Guadalajara?
   A: February.   B: July.
   C: August.   D: December.

2. (   ) The rainfall in May _____.
   A: is more than the rainfall in June
   B: is the same as the rainfall in November
   C: is about 150 mm
   D: is about 25 mm

3. (   ) For how many months is the rainfall below 100 mm?
   A: One.   B: Four.
   C: Eight.   D: Twelve.

4. (   ) What is a good month for Jill and Steven to travel?
   A: March.
   B: July.
   C: September.
   D: October.

Grammar

Write the correct word in each blank.

1. Last year August _____ the wettest month.
   (is/was)

2. In 2005 a lot of rain _____ in July.
   (fall/fell)

3. Two years ago, May was _____ than April.
   (wetter/wettest)

4. Last July, Miami _____ a lot of rain.
   (get/got)

40 Tai Chi

Tai Chi is an ancient form of exercise. Millions of people around the world practice it. Tai Chi involves slow movements of the arms, legs, and body. Each movement helps exercise different muscles. The most common type of Tai Chi is the Yang style.

Tai Chi helps balance the body and mind. It makes them both strong. Tai Chi looks easy to do, but it is not. People have to practice for years to become good at it.

Vocabulary

Write the correct word in each blank.

| common | balance | exercise | body | muscles |

1. Most people try to _____ work and fun in their lives.

2. After such a long walk, all of my _____ are tired.

3. Playing sports is a good way to _____.

4. Heavy traffic is a _____ problem in many cities.

Reading

Choose the best answer.

1. (   ) Tai Chi is a _____ kind of exercise.
    A: new   B: fast
    C: slow   D: modern

2. (   ) Tai Chi is good for _____.
    A: older people only
    B: just a few of the body's muscles
    C: people in very few countries
    D: the body and mind

3. (   ) What is the Yang style?
    A: A popular style of Tai Chi.
    B: A movement.
    C: A muscle.
    D: A fast exercise.

4. (   ) What do we learn about Tai Chi?
    A: It's impossible to learn.
    B: It takes time to learn it well.
    C: Everybody is good at it.
    D: Most of its movements are for the arms.

Grammar

Write the correct word in each blank.

1. Each _____ is different.
    (movement/movements)

2. There are many _____ in the _____.
    (muscle/muscles)   (body/bodies)

3. This type of _____ is not easy.
    (exercises/exercise)

4. Millions of _____ practice Tai Chi.
    (people/peoples)

Answer Key

Unit 1

Vocabulary
1. visit
2. along
3. side
4. Both

Reading
1. C   2. D
3. B   4. C

Grammar
1. The two falls are on the Niagara River
2. Both falls are very powerful.
3. The first is called Horseshoe Falls.
4. The second is called American Falls.

Unit 2

Vocabulary
1. secret
2. introduce
3. choose
4. picture

Reading
1. A   2. A
3. B   4. B

Grammar
1. Each   2. Some
3. Others   4. All

Unit 3

Vocabulary
1. country
2. excellent
3. rule
4. simple

Reading
1. C   2. A
3. A   4. D

Grammar
1. The players are tall and skillful.
2. He plays basketball and football.
3. Lisa and Carol play for the Tigers.

Unit 4

Vocabulary
1. time
2. So far
3. lab
4. great

Reading
1. D   2. B
3. C   4. B

Grammar
1. D   2. C
3. A   4. B

Unit 5

Vocabulary
1. class
2. wake up
3. neighborhood
4. break

Reading
1. D   2. D
3. C   4. D

Grammar
1. day
2. afternoon
3. weekend
4. mornings

Unit 6

Vocabulary
1. habit
2. spread
3. shower
4. health

Reading
1. C 2. A
3. D 4. A

Grammar
1. sleeping
2. exercising
3. doing
4. going

Unit 7

Vocabulary
1. team
2. information
3. photograph
4. inside

Reading
1. A 2. A
3. D 4. D

Grammar
1. Is
2. are
3. Am
4. is

Unit 8

Vocabulary
1. spend
2. narrow
3. delicious
4. friendly

Reading
1. B 2. A
3. C 4. A

Grammar
1. Does the city have many museums?
2. It has many famous temples.
3. We don't have time to see everything.
4. She doesn't have a picture of the city.

Unit 9

Vocabulary
1. river
2. department store
3. street
4. supermarket

Reading
1. D 2. A
3. D 4. B

Grammar
1. Turn left at the next street.
2. The bank is across the street from here.
3. Is there a restaurant near here?

Unit 10

Vocabulary
1. appreciate
2. total
3. plastic
4. out of

Reading
1. B 2. B
3. A 4. A

Grammar
1. Will you give me a plastic bag?
2. He will bring his own bags.
3. He can't give him a bag.
4. Can he change a twenty?

Answers

Unit 11

Vocabulary
1. save
2. communicate
3. group
4. ocean

Reading
1. C 2. D
3. B 4. A

Grammar
1. There were more than 100 in one group.
2. They can live up to 40 years.
3. They usually don't live more than 40 years.
4. There were not more than 10 in the other group.

Unit 12

Vocabulary
1. dinner
2. children
3. office
4. subway

Reading
1. D 2. B
3. D 4. C

Grammar
1. He doesn't work in the subway station.
2. He doesn't take the bus to work.
3. He doesn't go home at 6:00.
4. He doesn't spend time with his friends.

Unit 13

Vocabulary
1. deal   2. waiter
3. customer   4. salad

Reading
1. D 2. C
3. B 4. A

Grammar
1. You can have a cheese pizza or a sausage pizza.
2. You can have a large soup or a small soup.
3. You can have iced tea or coffee.

Unit 14

Vocabulary
1. beautiful
2. city
3. enjoy
4. mountain

Reading
1. B 2. A
3. B 4. C

Grammar
1. D 2. C
3. A 4. B

Unit 15

Vocabulary
1. advice   2. Everybody
3. plenty of   4. catch a cold

Reading
1. C 2. D
3. B 4. A

Grammar
1. C 2. B
3. D 4. A

Unit 16

Vocabulary
1. meal
2. piece
3. need
4. ready

Reading
1. A   2. D
3. B   4. B

Grammar
1. First
2. Second
3. Next
4. Finally

Unit 17

Vocabulary
1. roll of film
2. time
3. tax
4. telephone

Reading
1. C   2. C
3. B   4. C

Grammar
1. rolls of wrap
2. gifts
3. DVDs
4. boxes of candy

Unit 18

Vocabulary
1. members
2. similar
3. display
4. activities

Reading
1. B   2. A
3. B   4. B

Grammar
1. Our club meets twice a month.
2. Can I join your hiking club?
3. Their computer club doesn't have many members.

Unit 19

Vocabulary
1. dawn
2. relatives
3. lie
4. pray

Reading
1. B   2. A
3. C   4. D

Grammar
1. During
2. After
3. During
4. After

Unit 20

Vocabulary
1. different
2. interesting
3. favorite
4. hard

Reading
1. B   2. A
3. B   4. C

Grammar
1. C. It's ours.
2. D. It's his.
3. B. It's theirs.
4. A. It's hers.

Answers

Unit 21

Vocabulary
1. full-time
2. building
3. kitchen
4. living room

Reading
1. A   2. D
3. D   4. C

Grammar
1. We do not live in a three-story apartment.
2. It does not have a fully-furnished living room.
3. It does not have a very large kitchen.

Unit 22

Vocabulary
1. international
2. dangerous
3. hurt
4. Action

Reading
1. A   2. D
3. A   4. C

Grammar
1. often
2. sometimes
3. never
4. often

Unit 23

Vocabulary
1. swimming
2. Sometimes
3. weather
4. puppy

Reading
1. D   2. A
3. B   4. A

Grammar
1. Is my sister swimming with Jeff?
   Is Jeff swimming with my sister?
2. Are you enjoying the hot weather?
3. What are you doing this summer?

Unit 24

Vocabulary
1. fast   2. anybody
3. line   4. Slow down

Reading
1. B   2. C
3. B   4. A

Grammar
1. How fast does he walk?
2. How long does he wait?
3. How fast does he speak?
4. How far can he go?

Unit 25

Vocabulary
1. price   2. budget
3. tie   4. kind of

Reading
1. D   2. D
3. B   4. A

Grammar
1. B   2. D
3. A   4. C

Unit 26

Vocabulary
1. ticket
2. expensive
3. comfortable
4. travel

Reading
1. D   2. A
3. B   4. D

Grammar
1. more
2. more
3. faster
4. less

Unit 27

Vocabulary
1. cause
2. thirsty
3. Unfortunately
4. fly

Reading
1. C   2. D
3. B   4. B

Grammar
1. don't
2. does
3. doesn't
4. do

Unit 28

Vocabulary
1. finish
2. date
3. boss
4. cancel

Reading
1. B   2. C
3. A   4. A

Grammar
1. I have to make so many calls.
2. I have to send a lot of emails.
3. But I don't have to cancel my date.

Unit 29

Vocabulary
1. directions
2. invite
3. birthday
4. celebrate

Reading
1. A   2. A
3. C   4. C

Grammar
1. for
2. to
3. for, to
4. for

Unit 30

Vocabulary
1. check
2. plans
3. newspaper
4. help

Reading
1. A   2. B
3. D   4. D

Grammar
1. We need to make some plans.
2. I don't need to work after five.
3. Do you need to check the paper?

Answers

Unit 31

Vocabulary
1. capital
2. million
3. natural
4. foreign

Reading
1. B   2. C
3. B   4. D

Grammar
1. Mexico City is the capital of Mexico.
2. Is Mexico City also the heart of the economy?
3. The city is the home of many people.

Unit 32

Vocabulary
1. chatroom
2. website
3. Internet
4. search

Reading
1. A   2. B
3. D   4. C

Grammar
1. from
2. on
3. in
4. in

Unit 33

Vocabulary
1. usually
2. library
3. smile
4. way

Reading
1. B   2. B
3. D   4. C

Grammar
1. much   2. many
3. many   4. much

Unit 34

Vocabulary
1. valuable   2. learn
3. feeling   4. museum

Reading
1. A   2. D
3. C   4. B

Grammar
1. Some things are really valuable.
2. Everything in her house is an antique.
3. The museum has something for everybody.

Unit 35

Vocabulary
1. restaurant
2. own
3. taste
4. weekend

Reading
1. C   2. A
3. D   4. D

Grammar
1. He goes to the restaurant and does his homework there.
2. Does he clean the tables and help in the kitchen?
3. He goes there after school and on weekends.

Unit 36

Vocabulary
1. sorry
2. problem
3. message
4. urgent

Reading
1. C   2. B
3. D   4. A

Grammar
1. D   2. A
3. B   4. C

Unit 37

Vocabulary
1. during
2. business
3. custom
4. culture

Reading
1. C   2. A
3. D   4. B

Grammar
1. Not all of Spain follows this custom.
2. Not every business closes its doors.
3. Not many people take a siesta.

Unit 38

Vocabulary
1. famous or special
2. young
3. life
4. pressure

Reading
1. A   2. B
3. D   4. D

Grammar
1. C   2. D
3. B   4. A

Unit 39

Vocabulary
1. average
2. important
3. prefer
4. plan

Reading
1. B   2. D
3. C   4. A

Grammar
1. was   2. fell
3. wetter   4. got

Unit 40

Vocabulary
1. balance
2. muscles
3. exercise
4. common

Reading
1. C   2. D
3. A   4. B

Grammar
1. movement
2. muscles, body
3. exercise
4. people

For the Teacher • Read 75

Series Format

This book is the second in a series of four readers called The Read and Learn Series for beginning-level students. There are 40 units in each book. The readings in this book average about 75 words in length, and a total of just over 700 different words are used in the 40 readings. A summary of the series is below:

Book One: Read 50
50-Word Reading Passages
at the 600-word level

Book Two: Read 75
75-Word Reading Passages
at the 700-word level

Book Three: Read 100
100-Word Reading Passages
at the 800-word level

Book Four: Read 125
125-Word Reading Passages
at the 900-word level

The simple and easy-to-use units follow the same two-page format in all four volumes. A reading is followed by three short exercises that correlate with and expand upon the topical and linguistic content in the reading. Answers to the exercises are found at the back of the book.

The content of the units is broad and comprehensive in its appeal and may be used by learners from middle school to community college, and even beyond.

Reading Passages

The readings in the books include a variety of written material: articles, stories, conversations, menus, charts, diagrams, schedules, and Internet pages and messages. The readings are intended to be entertaining, informative, and useful. They focus on the various reading skills required for living and learning in our contemporary English-speaking world. They are international in scope to stimulate interest in and knowledge of other places and cultures, from the Amazon to Mount Fuji, and to emphasize that English is an international language.

Exercises

Following each reading there are **three types of exercises.** The first is a simple multiple choice exercise that focuses on the meaning and use of selected **vocabulary** items from the reading. In general, the items are used in a context that is somewhat different from the context in the reading. The **reading** exercise checks the students' comprehension of the reading. It requires the students to find specific information and to infer additional, more implicit meanings in the text. The **grammar** exercise expands on a grammatical point (ex: pronoun forms, verb tenses, plurality) or grammatical structure (ex: word order, subject-verb agreement) encountered in the reading. All three exercises require the students to examine the details of the reading passage.

Using the Books

The format of the four-book series is simple and easy to use, allowing for its use by individuals working in an independent mode or by students in a teacher-guided formal class.

Independent Study Mode.

The answers in the back of the book allow learners to work on their language skills completely independently or to use the material as a supplement to a formal study program. The 160 units in the complete series give self-studying learners sufficient material for several hours of study. The progression of the units from short to longer passages provides controlled challenge and comprehensible input. As the passages increase in length and in vocabulary level, the learners' "known" language also increases to meet the challenge of dealing with the "unknowns" of the passages. The uniformity of the units allows the learners the opportunity to focus on the language and not waste time trying to figure out what to do from unit to unit. Most important, perhaps, by following through the entire series, the learners will experience the satisfaction of feeling and recognizing progress.

Formal Class Mode.

Using the books as part of ongoing class work can be done in a variety of ways. A simple and effective procedure is outlined below:

1) Pre-reading preparation. Introduce the nature of the topic and engage the students in a discussion or question-answer session that activates what they may already know about the topic.

2) Initial, silent reading. The students read the passage silently with (or without, as you prefer) their dictionaries to gain an overall understanding. Depending on the level of the class, one to three minutes should be sufficient for this.

3) Reading aloud. This can be done by the teacher, or by students taking turns. A pause for questions and clarification can be added after each sentence or only after the entire passage.

4) Doing the exercises. This can be done individually, but it is often more effective to pair the students and have them work cooperatively. Simply put, two heads are better than one, and the practice of working and learning together can be a very valuable learning experience in itself.

5) Checking the answers. Self-checking or paired checking may generate some questions which should be clarified either as a whole-class activity or as the teacher circulates and responds to individuals or pairs.

6) Discussion. A teacher-led or small group discussion of the content gives the students the opportunity to use the language they already command to talk about new information with newly acquired knowledge and skill (new words, phrases, structures).

7) Writing. The students can keep a notebook or journal and record a sentence or two ("Today, I learned . ."), or perhaps a paragraph stimulated by the reading. An alternative is to do a short dictation using sentences based on the information in the reading.

Semi-Independent Study.

The material can be used in a formal program by having the students read the material and do the exercises out of class. For example, a unit is assigned for homework, and is followed by a brief review the next day. An alternative is a teacher-made quiz to keep the students on task.

Using the CD

A CD is available for each book. It is an optional element, but its use may provide an important and valuable extra dimension to the reading program. Obviously, the CD offers an opportunity for the students to hear a standard pronunciation and phrasing of the text. This can be a very important supplement to an independent study mode, and it may also be very useful in a setting where the teacher's own pronunciation is too heavily influenced by their native language. The CD can also be used to work on listening comprehension. It can be played in class before or after the reading, or the students can follow along by looking at the text as they listen.

Legends: 52 People Who Made a Difference

Graded readings from American history – beginner to intermediate. There are 13 units, each with four readings of 100, 150, 200, and 250 words. The legendary people covered in the units are folk heroes, Civil War and anti-slavery heroes, Native Americans, inventors and scientists, educators and reformers, adventures, human rights leaders, business and labor leaders, famous presidents, military leaders and heroes, writers, entertainers, and sports heroes. Personal and historical timelines are designed to controlled practice of language structures and to stimulate conversation about American culture and history. CD available.

American Holidays: Exploring Traditions, Customs, & Backgrounds

An intermediate reader explaining each of the official national holidays, three cultural holidays (Chinese New Year, Kwanzaa, and Cinco de Mayo), and Christian, Muslim, and Jewish religious holidays. Exercises practice vocabulary building skills, discussion, and Web research. CD available.

Surveys for Conversation

48 surveys designed for beginning to intermediate students – before class they read the surveys and fill them out with their personal information and opinions. In class they enjoy lively conversations which everyone is prepared to participate in. Topics include family, friendship, pets, shopping, clothes, TV, music, computers, space, celebrations, love, marriage, birth & death, work, books, health, summer, winter, crime, war & peace, AD 2100, and the environment.

Do As I Say: Operations, Procedures, and Rituals

A TPR classic revised and updated. Fun activities are ideal for building vocabulary, confidence with grammar, and accuracy in giving and taking instructions.

The Sanchez Family: Now, Tomorrow, and Yesterday

A first book for beginning ESl/EFL students which in a few pages teaches there survival tenses: present progressive, going-to future, and past.

English Interplay

Beginning to intermediate texts for basic English, focused primarily on interactive activities in the classroom using many different approaches and techniques to build vocabulary and all language skills.

To order or for information on these and other materials, contact

www.ProLinguaAssociates.com or 800-366-4775